margarita
martini
mojito

margarita
martini
mojito

hamlyn   Allan Gage

Notes

While the advice and information in this book is believed to be accurate, neither the author nor the publisher will be responsible for any injury, losses, damages, actions, proceedings, claims, demands, expenses and costs (including legal costs) incurred or in any way arising out of following the recipes in this book.

The measure that has been used in the recipes is based on a bar jigger, which is 25 ml (1 fl oz).

The Department of Health advises that eggs should not be consumed raw. This book contains recipes made with raw eggs. It is prudent for more vulnerable people to avoid these recipes.

First published in Great Britain in 2006 by Hamlyn,
a division of Octopus Publishing Group Ltd,
2–4 Heron Quays, London E14 4JP

ISBN-13: 978-0-600-61514-9
ISBN-10: 0-600-61514-6

A CIP catalogue record for this book is available from the British Library

Printed and bound in China

10 9 8 7 6 5 4 3 2 1

Contents

6 Introduction

10 Margaritas

34 Martinis

70 Mojitos

94 Index

96 Acknowledgements

Introduction

If you're a cocktail connoisseur, chances are you've sipped on a margarita, martini or mojito in the past. These three drinks are among the most popular on any cocktail menu, and this is partly due to their classic, timeless nature. However, it's their versatility that gives them universal appeal, with variations on the traditional mixes making them easily adaptable to every taste and occasion.

This book brings together many exciting interpretations of these cocktails so that you can test out your bartending skills and learn how to create everything from a Dry Martini (page 36) to a Mosquito Mojito (page 90) or the party favourites, Margarita Jellies (page 33).

Making history

Every cocktail has a story to tell, and the margarita, martini and mojito are no exceptions. Their origins date back well over a hundred years and during that time they have gradually developed and evolved into the drinks we know and love today.

It is generally believed that the first margarita was mixed in Mexico, although stories vary as to its exact origins. One credits the invention of the drink to the hostess of a swanky pool party, while another tells of a showgirl who had an allergy to all alcohol except tequila. She wanted something a little adventurous to sip on, and a creative bartender obliged by coming up with the margarita.

The town of Martinez in California stakes its claim as the birthplace of the martini. However, a bartender and several drinkers with names similar to that of the great cocktail have also been credited with being either the inventor or the inspiration for the drink. It is generally accepted that the martini has evolved over the years and previous incarnations have included various different combinations of spirits and garnishes that eventually led to the modern dry martini.

The mojito's beginnings were far from glamorous, because this drink that combined sugar cane and unrefined rum was originally made by slaves in Cuba. The combination proved to be a popular one and the mojito was born. It soon became the drink of choice on the island and the speciality at the famous La Bodeguita del Medio bar in Havana, where the rich and famous gathered to socialize. In fact, the mojito is often cited as being the favourite tipple of Ernest Hemingway, who regularly drank there.

Margarita

With its fun-loving image and reputation as a party drink, the margarita is open to plenty of adventurous variations, which has seen it enjoy a resurgence of popularity in recent years. However, despite the exotic name, the classic margarita

comprises just three main ingredients: tequila, triple sec and lime juice.

Although the classic recipe remains popular, this is often adapted to include fruit or spices and has resulted in drinks such as the Key Lime Margarita (page 26) and Cancun's Finest (page 21). Frozen margaritas (pages 14 and 30) have also become a popular drink and are a great party choice as they can be prepared in advance.

Martini

The martini is undoubtedly the most famous cocktail of them all. It's the drink of choice for the glamorous set and has a suave, sophisticated image. Like the margarita, the cocktail itself is a simple combination of ingredients – in this case vermouth and gin – that are prepared in a specific way. Purists insist that the vermouth be merely swirled around the glass then discarded before the gin is added. An olive garnish often provides the finishing touch and is dropped into the cocktail for a hint of another flavour.

Mojito

Sugar, mint leaves, lime juice, rum and soda water are the ingredients for this refreshing cocktail that's a favourite in bars the world over. The mojito is as enjoyable to prepare as it is to drink, and it's a great cocktail to include if you're planning a party. The process of combining the sugar, mint and lime is called 'muddling', and this really is the key to the success of the cocktail.

Taking stock

It's good to keep your bar well stocked with all the basics you're likely to need for preparing your favourite cocktails. If you're planning a party, look through the recipes in advance and choose a

few drinks to prepare for your guests. That way you'll have all the right ingredients and won't get flustered by trying to mix too many different drinks on the night. Your basic MMM (margarita, martini, mojito) bar should include the following items:

- **Spirits and liqueurs** tequila, gin, rum, vermouth, triple sec and vodka (if you prefer a vodka martini, or vodkatini)
- **Mixers** soda water and fruit juices
- **Flavourings** bitters, such as peach and orange

- **Garnishes** mint, berries, fruit slices, olives, salt, sugar; citrus fruit and cucumbers may be cut into wedges, wheels or twists.

A good selection of spirits, juices, mixers and fruit should cover most of the cocktails in this book, but certain recipes will require more unusual ingredients, such as peach schnapps and passion fruit, so double-check that you have everything before you start mixing. You'll also need plenty of ice, both in cubes and crushed, and it's a good idea to get some prepared in advance, or buy a couple of bags to keep in the freezer. As well as being used in crushed form in many of the recipes in this book, ice is also used in cubes to chill ingredients in the cocktail shaker as they're being combined and to keep glasses nice and cool while the drink is being prepared.

Margaritas

The
classic

This simple combination of punchy ingredients has made the classic margarita one of the most popular cocktails.

1¹/₂ measures silver tequila
1 measure fresh lime juice
1 measure Cointreau

Pour all the ingredients into a shaker and shake with cubed ice. Moisten the rim of a chilled coupette with a lime wedge and coat with fine rock salt on the outside of the rim. Double-strain the cocktail into the glass and decorate with a lime wheel.

Frozen
classic

A chilled-out version of the classic that's perfect for hot summer days in the garden.

1¹/₂ measures silver tequila
1 measure fresh lime juice
1 measure Cointreau

Pour all the ingredients into a blender and add a small scoop of crushed ice. If desired, moisten the rim of a chilled coupette with a lime wedge and coat with fine rock salt on the outside of the rim. Blend the cocktail, adding more ice. Double-strain the cocktail into the glass and decorate with a lime wedge.

The
grand

This indulgent drink has a rich appearance and depth of flavour.

$1^1/_2$ measures gold tequila
1 measure fresh lime juice
1 measure Grand Marnier

Pour all the ingredients into a shaker and shake with cubed ice. Moisten the rim of a chilled coupette with a lime wedge and coat with fine rock salt on the outside of the rim only. Double-strain the cocktail into the glass and decorate with a lime wheel.

Incarita

This fruity little number uses raspberry purée for added sweetness and a dash of colour.

1¹/₂ measures aged (*anejo*) tequila
1 measure fresh lime juice
¹/₂ measure Cointreau
¹/₂ measure raspberry purée
¹/₂ measure Chambord

Build up all the ingredients over crushed ice in a highball glass, stir and add a little more crushed ice. Garnish with a few raspberries and serve with long straws.

Passion fruit

Let your passions run free with this exotic cocktail that includes fresh passion fruit and syrup.

1 passion fruit
1¹/₂ measures silver tequila
1 measure fresh lime juice
¹/₂ measure Cointreau
¹/₂ measure passion-fruit syrup

Squeeze half the passion-fruit flesh into a shaker and add the remaining ingredients. Shake with cubed ice and double-strain into a chilled coupette. Squeeze the remaining passion-fruit flesh into the drink.

Elderflower
& peach

An unusual combination of flavours that results in a drink that is both delicate and distinctive.

1¹/₂ measures silver tequila
1 measure fresh lime juice
¹/₂ measure Cointreau
¹/₂ measure peach schnapps
¹/₄ measure elderflower cordial

Pour all the ingredients into a shaker and shake with cubed ice. Double-strain into a chilled cocktail glass and decorate with an edible flower.

Cancun's finest

Named after Mexico's party destination, the melon liqueur gives this cocktail a beach bar feel.

4 chunks watermelon
$1/2$ measure fresh lime juice
dash melon syrup
$1^1/2$ measures silver tequila
$1/2$ measure Midori

Muddle the watermelon chunks with the lime juice and melon syrup in the base of a Boston shaker, add the tequila and Midori then shake with cubed ice. Double-strain into a chilled cocktail glass and decorate with a slice of watermelon.

Lavender

This unusual drink makes use of the distinctive scent of dried lavender.

5 raspberries
6 blueberries
$^1/_2$ measure lime cordial
$1^1/_2$ measures silver tequila
$^1/_2$ measure triple sec
dash coconut cream
$^1/_4$ measure dried lavender buds

Muddle the berries and cordial in the base of a Boston shaker, add all the remaining ingredients and shake with cubed ice. Double-strain into a chilled cocktail glass and decorate with a purple rose petal.

Tijuana

The blackcurrant cassis and the Xante pear liqueur combine to produce a riot of flavours.

1¹/₂ measures silver tequila
¹/₂ measure crème de cassis
¹/₂ measure fresh lime juice
¹/₂ measure Xante pear liqueur

Pour all the ingredients into a shaker and shake with cubed ice. Double-strain into a chilled cocktail glass and decorate with a lime twist.

Key lime

If you've got a sweet tooth, this decadent drink will be a real favourite.

1¹/₂ measures silver tequila
1 measure fresh lime juice
¹/₂ measure lime cordial
¹/₂ measure Cointreau
¹/₂ measure lime curd
whipped cream

Pour all the liquid ingredients into a blender with the lime curd and a small scoop of crushed ice. Blend until smooth and serve in a chilled coupette. Put a layer of cream on top and garnish with some lime twists and blueberries.

Cinnamon
& orange

A classic combination of strong flavours results in a cocktail to remember.

1¹/₂ measures silver tequila
1 measure fresh lime juice
¹/₂ measure orange Curaçao
¹/₂ measure cinnamon syrup
ground cinnamon

Pour all the liquid ingredients into a shaker and shake with cubed ice. Double-strain into a chilled cocktail glass. Sprinkle the ground cinnamon through a flame over the surface of the drink.

40 licks

Tangy citrus and sweet vanilla provide a real workout for the taste buds.

1 lime
$^1/_2$ measure Madagascan vanilla syrup
$1^1/_2$ measures silver tequila
$^1/_2$ measure Licor 43 (citrus and vanilla liqueur)

Muddle the lime with the vanilla syrup in the base of a rocks glass and add a scoop of crushed ice. Pour over the tequila and Licor 43, stir, and add a little more crushed ice. Garnish with lime wedges and serve with short straws.

Frozen
strawberry

Strawberries make a wonderful addition to a margarita and the Cointreau blends perfectly.

$1/4$ measure silver tequila
1 measure fresh lime juice
$1/2$ measure Cointreau
$1/2$ measure strawberry syrup
5 strawberries

Pour all the ingredients into a blender and add a small scoop of crushed ice. Blend until smooth and serve in a large chilled coupette, garnished with a strawberry slices.

Margarita jellies

These jellies are the ultimate party shots – and easy to prepare in advance, too.

½ block raspberry jelly
4 measures hot water
4 measures silver tequila
2 measures fresh lime juice
2 measures sugar syrup
cinnamon-infused whipped cream

Melt the jelly with the hot water in a bowl and add the remaining liquid ingredients. Stir thoroughly and divide between 10 shot glasses. Place in the refrigerator and leave for at least 6 hours or until set. Serve with scoops of the cream and small spoons.

Martinis

Dry

This traditional dry martini is flavoured with orange bitters and dry vermouth.

$1/2$ measure dry vermouth
4 drops orange bitters
$2^1/2$ measures gin

Fill a mixing glass with ice cubes and add the vermouth and orage bitters. Stir until the ice cubes are thoroughly coated then pour off the excess. Pour in the gin and stir thoroughly then strain the cocktail into a chilled glass. Drop a few olives into the drink.

Dry classic

Sometimes called the naked martini, this cocktail is far drier than the original dry martini.

1/2 measure dry vermouth
3 measures frozen gin

Swirl the vermouth around the inside of a chilled cocktail glass then discard the excess. Pour in the frozen gin and add an olive or a lemon twist.

Gimlet

This is a sweeter martini with a pronounced citrus flavour from the lime cordial.

2 measures gin
1 measure lime cordial
$1/2$ measure water, to taste
lime wedge

Pour the gin and lime cordial into a mixing glass, fill up with ice cubes and stir well. Strain into a chilled cocktail glass and add water to taste, then squeeze the lime wedge into the cocktail before placing it in the drink.

White
lady

Star fruit is not a classic cocktail decoration, but it adds a distinctive touch to this quite sour martini.

1½ measures gin
¾ measure Cointreau
1 measure fresh lime juice
¼ measure sugar syrup
1 egg white

Pour all the ingredients into a shaker and shake well with cubed ice. Strain into a chilled cocktail glass and decorate with a thin slice of star fruit.

Smoky

A single measure of sloe gin adds a wonderful flavour to a traditional martini.

¹/₄ measure dry vermouth
2 measures gin
1 measure sloe gin
5 drops orange bitters

Put some ice cubes into a mixing glass, add the vermouth and stir until the ice cubes are well coated. Pour in the remaining ingredients and stir well, then strain into a chilled cocktail glass and add an orange twist.

Aviation

This sweet-and-sour martini has a lingering flavour and a pleasant tang from the Maraschino.

2¹/₂ measures gin
1¹/₂ measures fresh lemon juice
¹/₂ measure Maraschino
¹/₄ measure sugar syrup

Pour all the ingredients into a shaker and shake well with cubed ice. Strain into a chilled cocktail glass and add a lemon twist.

Saketini

Japanese sake is combined here with orange Curaçao to produce a martini with a beautifully aromatic edge.

2¹/₂ measures sake
1 measure vodka
¹/₂ measure orange Curaçao

Pour all the ingredients into a mixing glass and stir well with some cubed ice. Strain into a chilled cocktail glass and add two cucumber wheels.

Opal

The taste of fresh orange juice is emphasized by the intense and powerful orange flavour of the Cointreau.

2 measures gin
1 measure Cointreau
2 measures fresh orange juice

Pour all the ingredients into a shaker and shake well with cubed ice. Strain into a chilled cocktail glass. Drape a long twist of orange rind into the drink in a swirl.

Cosmopolitan

Dating from the mid-1990s, this is a perfect combination of fresh fruity flavours.

1^1/$_2$ measures citron vodka
1 measure Cointreau
1^1/$_2$ measures cranberry juice
^{1}/$_4$ measure fresh lime juice

Pour all the ingredients into a shaker and shake well with cubed ice. Strain into a chilled cocktail glass and add a flamed orange twist.

White
elephant

Simple and smooth, the blend of vodka and crème de cacao gives this creamy cocktail a powerful punch.

1¹/₂ measures vodka
1 measure white crème de cacao
1 measure single cream
¹/₄ measure full-cream milk

Pour all the ingredients into a shaker and shake well with cubed ice. Strain into a chilled cocktail glass.

Bellinitini

The combination of peach flavours and a generous serving of vodka makes this a very special drink.

2 measures vodka
$^1/_2$ measure peach purée
$^1/_2$ measure peach schnapps
4 drops peach bitters

Pour all the ingredients into a shaker and shake well with cubed ice. Strain into a martini glass and decorate with peach wedges.

French

This creamy martini blend, sweetened by the pineapple juice, is a real sweet treat.

2 measures vodka
1/2 measure Chambord
1 measure pineapple juice

Pour all the ingredients into a shaker and shake vigorously with cubed ice. Strain into a chilled martini glass and float a raspberry on top.

Chocotini

This is much sweeter than a normal martini, with rich, dark chocolate overtones.

2 measures vodka
1 measure dark crème de cacao
1/4 measure sugar syrup
1/2 measure chocolate syrup

Pour all the ingredients into a shaker and shake well with cubed ice. Swirl some extra chocolate syrup into a cocktail glass and strain in the cocktail.

Watermelon

The basil adds a fresh take on this classic drink, while the watermelon gives a fruity finish.

4 chunks watermelon
4 basil leaves
$1/2$ measure sugar syrup
2 measures gin

Muddle the watermelon, basil and syrup in the base of a Boston shaker, add the gin and then shake with cubed ice. Double-strain into a chilled cocktail glass and then decorate with a basil sprig.

Strawberry

This cocktail is perfect for summer drinks, when you can enjoy the wonderful taste of fresh strawberries.

3 fresh strawberries
$1/4$ measure sirop de fraises (strawberry syrup)
$2^1/_2$ measures vodka
$1/4$ measure dry vermouth

Put the strawberries and sirop de fraises into a mixing glass and muddle together. Transfer to a cocktail shaker, add the remaining ingredients and shake well with cubed ice. Strain into a chilled cocktail glass and decorate with half a strawberry.

Rude
cosmopolitan

This tequila-based martini, with its delicious and subtle combination of fruit flavours, is deceptively powerful.

1¹/₂ measures gold tequila
1 measure Cointreau
1 measure cranberry juice
¹/₂ measure fresh lime juice

Pour all the ingredients into a shaker and shake well with cubed ice. Strain into a chilled cocktail glass and decorate with a flamed orange twist.

Lemon

A combination of lemon and orange flavours gives this martini a fresh and simple taste.

1^1/$_2$ measures citron vodka
1 measure fresh lemon juice
^{1}/$_4$ measure sugar syrup
^{1}/$_4$ measure Cointreau
3 drops orange bitters

Pour all the ingredients into a shaker and shake well with cubed ice. Strain into a chilled cocktail glass and decorate with a lemon slice.

Vanilla

The soft, mellow flavour of fresh vanilla makes this a very popular martini.

1 vanilla pod
$^1/_4$ measure vanilla syrup
$2^1/_2$ measures vanilla vodka
$^1/_4$ measure dry vermouth

Put the vanilla pod and vanilla syrup in a mixing glass and muddle together. Add the remaining ingredients and shake well with cubed ice. Strain into a chilled cocktail glass and serve.

Tre

This delicious rum-based martini has a subtle mingling of flavours.

2 measures Havana 3-year-old rum
$^1/_4$ measure Chambord
1 measure apple juice
$^1/_4$ measure sugar syrup

Put some ice cubes into a mixing glass, add all the ingredients and stir well. Strain into a chilled cocktail glass and add a lemon twist.

Pale
original

This is a sweet-and-sour cocktail with a long ginger and lime finish.

2 measures gold tequila
$1/2$ measure ginger syrup
$1/2$ measure fresh lime juice
1 measure guava juice

Pour all the ingredients into a shaker and shake well with cubed ice. Strain into a chilled cocktail glass and decorate with lime wedges.

Red
rum

Redcurrants provide the colour and aged rum packs a powerful flavour punch.

small handful redcurrants
$^1/_2$ measure sloe gin
2 measures Bacardi 8-year-old rum
$^1/_2$ measure lemon juice
$^1/_2$ measure vanilla syrup

Muddle the currants and sloe gin together in the base of a shaker. Add the remaining ingredients, shake well with cubed ice, then double-strain into a chilled cocktail glass. Decorate with a string of redcurrants.

Royale

This celebratory cocktail is made in the glass using frozen vodka.

2¹/₂ measures frozen vodka
¹/₄ measure crème de cassis
Champagne, to top up

Pour the vodka into a chilled cocktail glass then stir in the crème de cassis. Top up with Champagne then decorate with a lemon twist.

Glamour

This fruity cocktail lives up to its name, with blood orange juice giving it a vibrant appearance.

1¹/₂ measures vodka
¹/₂ measure cherry brandy
2 measures blood orange juice
¹/₂ measure lime juice

Pour all the ingredients into a shaker and shake well with cubed ice. Strain into a chilled cocktail glass and decorate with twists of orange and lime.

Mojitos

Classic

Cuba was the birthplace of this cocktail with the ultimate sweet-and-sour combination.

$^1/_2$ lime
6–8 mint leaves
2 tsp granulated sugar
dash sugar syrup
2 measures gold rum
dash soda water

Muddle the first 4 ingredients in the base of a highball glass and add a scoop of crushed ice. Add the rum and stir while topping with soda, then garnish with a mint sprig.

Apple
soaked

Fresh apple juice and granulated sugar make perfect partners in this drink.

¹/₂ lime
6–8 mint leaves
2 tsp demerara sugar
2 measures white rum
2 measures fresh apple juice

Muddle the first 3 ingredients in the base of a highball glass and add a scoop of crushed ice. Add the rum and stir while topping with fresh apple juice. Finally, decorate with a mint sprig and 2 slices of red apple.

Limon

Lemon and orange make this
a refreshing citrus cocktail.

¹/₂ lime
2 slices lemon
2 slices orange
6–8 mint leaves
2 tsp granulated sugar
2 measures Bacardi limon rum
dash soda water

Muddle the first 5 ingredients in the
base of a highball glass and add a
scoop of crushed ice. Add the rum and
stir with a dash of soda. Finally, garnish
with a mint sprig and a slice of each of
the 3 citrus fruits.

Pink

It's the raspberry liqueur and cranberry juice that inspired the name of this drink.

¹/₂ lime
6–8 mint leaves
2 tsp sugar syrup
3 raspberries
2 measures white rum
¹/₂ measure Chambord
dash cranberry juice

Muddle the first 4 ingredients in the base of a highball glass and add a scoop of crushed ice. Add the rum and stir, then add the Chambord and top with the cranberry juice. Finally, decorate with a mint sprig.

Fidel's

It's unusual to see lager in a cocktail but here it's used to great effect.

1/2 lime
6–8 mint leaves
dash sugar syrup
2 measures white rum
dash lager

Muddle the first 3 ingredients in the base of a highball glass and add a scoop of crushed ice. Add the rum and stir, then top gradually with lager, being careful not to allow it to froth over, before garnishing with a mint sprig.

Raspberry

The raspberry syrup adds a distinctive colour and flavour to this summery mojito.

$1/_2$ lime
6–8 mint leaves
2 tsp granulated sugar
dash sugar syrup
1 measure raspberry purée
2 measures gold rum
dash soda water

Muddle the first 5 ingredients in the base of a highball glass and add a scoop of crushed ice. Add the rum and stir while topping with soda. Finally, decorate with 2 raspberries.

Ultimate
vanilla

Mint leaves, vanilla and aged rum combine to make a memorably moreish cocktail.

1/2 lime
6–8 mint leaves
2 tsp vanilla-infused demerara sugar
2 measures Bacardi 8-year-old rum
soda water, to taste

Muddle the first 3 ingredients in the base of a highball glass and add a scoop of crushed ice. Add the rum and stir, then add soda if required. Decorate with a mint sprig.

Pineapple

This will conjure up holiday memories and cheer you up on cold, wintry nights.

1/2 lime
6–8 mint leaves
4 pineapple chunks
2 tsp brown sugar
2 measures gold rum
dash pineapple juice

Muddle the first 4 ingredients in the base of a highball glass and add a scoop of crushed ice. Add the rum and stir until thoroughly mixed, then top with the pineapple juice. Decorate with a mint sprig and a few pineapple leaves.

Straight-up
double-strained

What could be more decadent than a Champagne cocktail? Save this for celebrations.

$^1/_2$ **measure fresh lime juice**
$^1/_2$ **measure strawberry purée**
6–8 mint leaves
2 tsp granulated sugar
2 measures gold rum
dash Champagne

Combine the first 5 ingredients in a shaker and shake well with cubed ice. Double-strain into a cocktail glass, add the Champagne and decorate with a few mint leaves.

Spiced

Rum provides spicy under-tones in this subtle variation of the classic mojito.

¹/₂ lime
6–8 mint leaves
2 tsp granulated sugar
dash sugar syrup
2 measures spiced rum
dash soda water

Muddle the first 4 ingredients in the base of a highball glass and add a scoop of crushed ice. Add the rum and stir while topping with soda, then add a mint sprig.

Bosito

Passion fruit and apple juice create this fruity cocktail.

2 measures Bacardi 8-year-old rum
1 measure passion-fruit purée
1 measure apple juice
dash sugar syrup
4 mint leaves

Pour all the ingredients into a shaker and shake well with cubed ice. Double-strain into a chilled cocktail glass and decorate with a grind of black pepper.

Campito

Bitter Campari is offset by sweet passion fruit syrup.

3 lime wedges
2 orange wedges
6–8 mint leaves
2 tsp granulated sugar
dash passion fruit syrup
2 measures gold rum
1/2 measure Campari
dash soda water

Muddle the first 5 ingredients in the base of a highball glass and add a scoop of crushed ice. Add the rum then the Campari, stirring after each addition, then add a little more crushed ice and top with soda. Finally, garnish with red berries.

Mosquito

Fruit and herbs make this cocktail a zingy, fresh treat for the palate.

¹/₂ lime
4 chunks watermelon
6–8 basil leaves
2 tsp granulated sugar
dash sugar syrup
2 measures gin
dash soda water

Muddle the first 5 ingredients in the base of a highball glass and add a scoop of crushed ice. Add the gin and stir, then add a little more crushed ice and finally the soda. Garnish with a watermelon wedge.

Strawberry
& passion fruit

This delicious fruit explosion
will get you in the party mood.

¹/₂ lime
6–8 mint leaves
2 tsp granulated sugar
dash passion fruit syrup
1 measure strawberry purée
2 measures gold rum
dash soda water

Muddle the first 5 ingredients in the
base of a highball glass and add a
scoop of crushed ice. Add the rum and
stir while topping with soda. Finally,
garnish with half a passion fruit.

Spiced **pear**

A double hit of pear in the form of purée and liqueur.

3 lime wedges
2 lemon wedges
6–8 mint leaves
2 tsp granulated sugar
dash sugar syrup
1 measure pear purée
1½ measures spiced rum
½ measure Xante pear liqueur
dash soda water

Muddle the first 6 ingredients in the base of a highball glass and add a scoop of crushed ice. Add the spiced rum and pear liqueur and top with more crushed ice. Stir while topping with soda. Finally, garnish with some skinless pear wedges.

Index

A

apple juice: Apple
Soaked 74
Mojito 87
Tre 64
Aviation 44

B

Bellinitini 52
blueberries: Lavender
Margarita 23
Bosito 87

C

Campari: Campito 89
Cancun's Finest 21
Chambord: French 53
Pink Mojito 77
Champagne: Royale 67
Chocotini 54
Cinnamon and Orange
Margarita 28
Classic Margarita 12
Classic Mojito 72
Cointreau: margaritas
12-14, 17-20, 27, 30
martinis 41, 47-8, 59-
60

Cosmopolitan 48
Rude Cosmopolitan
59
cranberry juice:
Cosmopolitans 48,
59
crème de cacao:
Chocotini 54
White Elephant 51
crème de cassis:
Royale 67
Tijuana 24
Curaçao: Cinnamon
and Orange
Margarita 28
Saketini 45

D

Dry Classic Martini 38
Dry Martini 36

E

Elderflower and Peach
Margarita 20

F

Fidel's 78
40 Licks 29

French 53
Frozen Classic
Margarita 14
Frozen Strawberry
Margarita 30

G

Gimlet 39
gin: martinis 36-44,
47, 57
Mosquito 90
Glamour 68
Grand Margarita 15
guava juice: Pale
Original 65

I

Incarita 17

J

jellies, Margarita 33

K

Key Lime Margarita 27

L

Lavender Margarita 23
lemon juice: Aviation

44
Lemon 60
Licor 43: 40 Licks 29
lime: Gimlet 39
margaritas 12-33
Straight-up Double-
strained Mojito 84
White Lady 41
Limon 75

M

Maraschino: Aviation
44
margaritas 6, 7-8, 11-33
Cancun's Finest 21
Cinnamon and
Orange 28
The Classic 12
Elderflower and
Peach 20
40 Licks 29
Frozen Classic 14
Frozen Strawberry
30
The Grand 15
Incarita 17
jellies 33
Key Lime 27

Lavender 23
Passion Fruit 18
Tijuana 24
martinis 7, 8, 35-69
  Aviation 44
  Bellinitini 52
  Chocotini 54
  Cosmopolitan 48
  Dry 36
  Dry Classic 38
  French 53
  Gimlet 39
  Glamour 68
  Lemon 60
  Opal 47
  Pale Original 65
  Red Rum 66
  Royale 67
  Rude Cosmopolitan
    59
  Saketini 45
  Smoky 42
  Strawberry 58
  Tre 64
  Vanilla 63
  Watermelon 57
  White Elephant 51
  White Lady 41
Midori: Cancun's
    Finest 21
mojitos 7, 8, 71-93
  Apple Soaked 74
  Bosito 87
  Campito 89

Classic 72
Fidel's 78
Limon 75
Mosquito 90
Pineapple 83
Pink 77
Raspberry 80
Spiced 86
Spiced Pear 92
Straight-up Double-
    strained 84
Strawberry and
    Passion Fruit 91
Ultimate Vanilla 81
Mosquito 90

O
Opal 47
orange juice: Glamour
    68
  Opal 47

P
Pale Original 65
passion fruit: Mojito 87
  Passion Fruit
    Margarita 18
  Strawberry and
    Passion Fruit
    Mojito 91
peach: Bellinitini 52
pear liqueur: Spiced
    Pear Mojito 92
pineapple: French 53

Pineapple Mojito 83
Pink Mojito 77

R
raspberries: Lavender
    Margarita 23
  Pink Mojito 77
  Raspberry Mojito 80
Red Rum 66
Royale 67
Rude Cosmopolitan 59
rum: mojitos 72-89,
    91-3
  Red Rum 66
  Tre 64

S
Saketini 45
sloe gin: Red Rum 66
  Smoky 42
Spiced Mojito 86
Spiced Pear Mojito 92
Straight-up Double-
    strained Mojito 84
strawberries: Frozen
    Strawberry
    Margarita 30
  Straight-up Double-
    strained Mojito 84
  Strawberry and
    Passion Fruit
    Mojito 91
  Strawberry Martini
    58

T
tequila: margaritas 12-
    33
  Pale Original 65
  Rude Cosmopolitan
    59
Tijuana 24
Tre 64
triple sec: Lavender
    Margarita 23

U
Ultimate Vanilla Mojito
    81

V
vanilla: Ultimate
    Vanilla Mojito 81
  Vanilla Martini 63
vermouth, martinis 36-
    8, 42, 58, 63
vodka, martinis 45, 48-
    54, 58, 60, 63, 67-9

W
watermelon: Cancun's
    Finest 21
  Mosquito 90
  Watermelon Martini
    57
White Elephant 51
White Lady 41

Acknowledgements

Photography © Octopus Publishing Group/Stephen Conroy
Drinks styling Allan Gage
Props stylist Sarah Waller
Executive editor Sarah Ford
Editor Emma Pattison
Executive art editor Joanna MacGregor
Designer Janis Utton
Senior production controller Martin Croshaw